until g
brush o
Cand
3 cups powd
8bsp. milk
tsp. almond
Mix

Christmas Traditions

Stories, Myths & Legends

[handwritten inscription: Jennifer — Celebrate proudly! cozy warm fires and sugar cookies! Ron 2021]

Ron Johnson

Photography by Jeffrey Sweet
Written by Ron Johnson & Claire Porter
Book Design by Heather Kane Kohler
Photography Assistant: Melanie Braun

© 2021 Ron Johnson

ISBN 978-0-578-97761-4

Contents

Introduction

I believe the best place for me to live and keep shop would be on the set of a Hallmark Christmas movie. I'm all about plaid, cozy warm fires, and I can never get enough sugar cookies! To have an opportunity to operate a business in a beautiful snow-covered village where there are always mugs of hot chocolate and Christmas carols sounds amazing.

As a shopkeeper with three specialty stores to tend to, people often assume that Christmas could be a hassle for me. That's not the case, though. There is never a day Christmas isn't on my mind. I truly can't wait to start flipping the stores as the season approaches. Once the stores are ready with their new look, it's time to get started at home! I'm a big believer in decorating early, which allows the decor to evolve with the season. At home, I find it best to leave as much of our existing decor in place as possible and simply accent around it. I find ways to reimagine decor, moving pieces around almost daily and discovering new ways to display cherished treasures

So many clients come into the stores feeling pressure to have the perfect holiday decor. I encourage them to choose items that speak to them, take them home and try placing them in different ways. I personally rarely buy anything with a specific spot in mind. I buy what I like and experiment until I find the perfect spot.

I've never been about the newest trends. I always enjoy building on our traditional Christmas collections, with their long-lasting charm and timeless appeal. I think it's sad that people won't use an object with sentimental meaning because they think it's not good enough to show off. Things around our home are far from perfect. Our trees are filled with hundreds of ornaments, and many have had some hard knocks through the years. My grandmother's ugly angel who is missing her wing or the deer with only one antler and one ear are all part of the story!

I enjoy telling stories through tablescapes and mantel decor. Whether it's a dining table on which Santa emerges from a snow-covered forest, a fresh arrangement reminiscent of an evening stroll through a garden, or a mantel of glistening finials clustered as though you're looking over a hillside dotted with church steeples, it's all part of a story — my very own Christmas story.

> *"I'm all about plaid, cozy warm fires, and I can never get enough sugar cookies!"*

Finials on a fireplace mantel mimic church steeples reaching high into the midnight sky.

Symbols of Christmas

Lean into the history and rich tradition of the season's most time-honored symbols. Recognizable holiday elements have their own story to tell, representing cherished religious stories and cultural traditions passed down for centuries.

The Christmas Star

The Christmas star is far more than a twinkling Christmas tree topper. In Biblical tradition, the radiant star of Bethlehem guided the three wise men to the birthplace of baby Jesus. Because of its pivotal role in the first Christmas story, the star's bright, shining light has come to represent the strength of the Christmas celebration. Associated with high thoughts and ideas, reflective stars bring bright light to Christmas decor and symbolize hope for good things to come. Much as the star of Bethlehem guided the wise men to the holy birth site, stars sprinkled throughout holiday compositions can guide the eye to delicate details and important accents.

Star finials and metallic ornaments in varying shapes, sizes and styles tell the story of gazing toward the heavens and seeing twinkling stars guiding you.

Rustic bark candles with moss tie into the candle's history as a tree adornment and make a stunning contrast to antique trophies.

Candles

andlelight brings Christmas alive in so many ways. The twinkling of light on a cold night warms the soul. Candles also have a spiritual element. They represent the guiding light of the star of Bethlehem, which is why they've long been a staple in Christmas decor. Starting in the 17th century, families used candles to light up the tree, and the tradition gradually spread around the world. At first, melted wax or pins held candles in place, but around 1890, candle holders for trees created a more secure way to bring glowing light to Christmas celebrations. Between 1902 and 1914, small lanterns and glass balls brought glimmers of light to tree branches. Not long after, department stores started replacing candles with string lights in their extravagant holiday displays. Although string lights are preferred for tree-lighting today, the charm and warmth of candles in decor instantly transports guests to days of yore when flickering lights adorned the tree and families gathered in celebration.

Holly

Holly has come to be associated most closely with Christmas as a religious symbol of eternal life. Holly appears in several religious traditions and is said to have been the thorned plant in Jesus' crown of thorns. Some stories even describe

white holly berries turning bright red because of Jesus' blood.

Outside of Christian tradition, ancient Romans and Greeks also regarded holly as a sacred shrub.

They were the first to deck their halls with boughs of holly because of the plant's deep green color, even through the harshest of winters. Representing goodwill and good fortune, holly wreaths were often sent as gifts to friends and family, especially to newlyweds. Greeting guests at the front door with a holly wreath can carry the spirit of good fortune into your home, and accents of holly can represent the hope of eternal life for loved ones.

A reminder of eternal
life, always-vibrant
holly pulled from the
yard comes together
with nandina berries
for a simple wreath.

Red & Green

Red and green have come to represent all things Christmas, and the pairing is not by accident. Like most Christmas symbols, these colors have roots in religious tradition, with red representing the blood of Jesus when he died on the cross. Green is tied to natural elements, symbolizing everlasting life. Not only does this color scheme show up in decor elements, but wintry flowers, pine trees and holly bushes naturally embody the colors of the season.

Using fresh pomegranates,
nandina berries clipped
from the yard and deep
red roses creates a punch
of red in an evergreen
arrangement

Nothing says traditional Christmas like red and green.

Antique green majolica plates with red Santa ornaments complement red candles in barley twist candle holders along with fresh pomegranates, berries, roses and winter greenery on a buffet.

Candy Canes

Few flavors are as universally tied to Christmas as the candy cane. Beyond being a beloved sweet treat, candy canes carry unique religious tradition. Some believe the curved shape represents the letter J for Jesus, while others insist that it's shaped after a shepherd's crook, representing Jesus' role as "The Good Shepherd." It has even been said that the red stripes represent Jesus' blood, and the white background stands for purity. Whether you enjoy them for their symbolism or for their fresh, festive flavor, candy canes are an instantly recognizable symbol of the season and bring a playful touch to your holiday decor.

A crisp white platter frames a swag of greenery that's made by combining candy cane ornaments in various textures. Beaded, glass and felt ornaments create a dynamic look.

Candy Cane Coffee Cake

Ingredients:
Coffee Cake
2 packages yeast
½ cup warm water (110–115°F)
2 cups sour cream, warmed
6 tablespoons butter, divided
1/3 cup sugar
2 eggs
2 teaspoons salt
5¾–6¼ cups all-purpose flour, divided
½ cup Maraschino cherries, chopped

Filling:
1 egg white
¾ cup confectioners sugar
½ cup almond paste, cubed

Candy Cane Glaze:
3 cups powdered sugar
6 tablespoons milk
½ teaspoon almond extract

Directions:
Preheat oven to 350°F. For filling, in a mixing bowl, beat egg white until foamy. Gradually add confectioners' sugar and almond paste. Beat until smooth and set aside.

In a separate bowl, dissolve yeast in warm water. Add sour cream, 4 tablespoons butter, sugar, eggs, salt and 2 cups flour. Beat until smooth. Stir in enough remaining flour to form a soft dough. Turn onto a floured surface and knead until smooth and elastic, about 6 to 8 minutes. Place in a greased bowl, turning once to grease top. Cover and let rise in a warm place until doubled, about 1 hour. Punch dough down. Turn onto a lightly floured surface and divide into thirds. Roll each portion into a 14-by-7-inch rectangle. On each long side, cut ¾ -inch wide strips about 2 inches into the center. Spread about 1/3 cup almond filling down the center of the rectangle. Spread ½ cup chopped Maraschino cherries on top of almond filling. Starting at one end, fold alternating strips at an angle across filling. Pinch ends to seal. Curve top. Place on a greased baking sheet. Bake at 350°F for 18 to 20 minutes or until golden brown. Melt remaining butter; brush over warm coffee cake.

While coffee cake is baking, prepare the glaze. Mix powdered sugar, milk and almond extract in a bowl. Drizzle glaze over cooled coffee cake in a swirled pattern.

Bells

Whether chiming from a church steeple, jingling alongside a sleigh, or ringing in song, bells play an important role in holiday celebrations. Ringing bells are said to proclaim the arrival of the Christmas season and announce the birth of Jesus. The most dynamic designs engage all five senses, and the sound of jingling bells can add an inviting sense of interaction and festivity to your decor.

Instead of opting for a themed tree, grouping ornament collections together highlights the various styles within your collection.

Evergreen Trees

With their undying branches and year-round vibrancy, evergreen trees represent everlasting hope and eternal life. That's why evergreens and their branches have been used in Christmas customs and winter solstice celebrations for centuries — even ancient Romans decorated houses with fir branches for the new year. According to legend, if you sit under a pine tree on Christmas Eve, you can hear angels singing. Decorating with unadorned branches and natural trees is a way to honor the natural beauty of these timeless Christmas symbols.

The Evolution of Santa

The jolly Santa Claus we know today evolved from centuries of lore about a magical man and his hoofed companions visiting homes and spreading Christmas cheer.

A Santa figurine made by Kansas City artist Connie Krizner is joined by a French majolica goat made in the 1880s by Jerome Massier.

The Christmas Goat

Long before Santa soared over rooftops in his sleigh, he strode into town atop the Christmas goat. In Sweden and other Scandinavian countries, Santa brought good tidings and bags of gifts while riding atop the Yule Goat, or Julbock. However, the goat hadn't always been a jolly figure. The Yule goat was originally tied to the grain harvest goat, a frightening figure who romped around on Christmas night, demanding food at villagers' doors. As Yule festivals grew in popularity in Northern Europe, the Christmas goat gradually dropped its scary connotation. Instead, he was said to help Santa deliver presents to the villages, and Santa was often depicted riding the goat and carrying gifts.

Santa brought good tidings and gifts while riding the Yule Goat.

By the 19th century, the Yule goat's role in the festivities grew. He began delivering presents to well behaved children on his own. Many fathers would dress as the Yule goat and hand out gifts to children and family members on Christmas day. In some areas, children would leave barley out as a treat for the goat, often putting it in a shoe. Over time, the responsibility of gift giving passed from the goat itself to mischievous elves who rode goats and left presents for sleeping children.

Eventually, the lore of gift-bearing elves gave way, and new stories emerged of Father Christmas bearing gifts. However, no matter the story, he always appeared with his trusty Yule goat at his side.

The Christmas Donkey

While Scandinavian Christmas stories had Father Christmas accompanied by goats, a different story was taking place in France. On the feast day of St. Nick on December 6th, St. Nick (called Père Noël) would descend from the sky on a flying donkey named Gui. The pair would quietly land on the rooftops of homes and slip down the chimney to leave bundles of gifts for well behaved children as they slept through the night.

In some stories, Gui walks along with Santa, carrying sacks and baskets of gifts. To thank the Christmas donkey for his hard work, French children would fill their shoes with carrots or apples and line them beside the fireplace as a snack for the beloved companion. After Gui polished off his treats, Santa would fill the empty little shoes with small gifts and sweets. This is still custom during the Festival of Saint Nicholas in some parts of Northern France.

Reindeer

By 1812, Christmas goats, donkeys and horses gave way to reindeer, which Santa found as his preferred transportation. Sleighs were a common method of travel in Europe around the time that reindeer started to appear in Christmas stories, and the popular transportation method was added to stories of St. Nick. In 1823 Clement C. Moore wrote the poem "A Visit from St. Nicholas," — more commonly known as "The Night Before Christmas" — and in it, Santa's sleigh was pulled by not just one reindeer, but eight! Moore's poem even named them all, but with some variations.

For example, Donner and Blitzen were originally called Dundere and Blixem, Dutch words for thunder and lightning.

Finally in 1949, Santa's sleigh-pulling roster of reindeer was complete with the addition of Rudolph. Robert May, an employee of department store Montgomery Ward, wanted to make a Christmas booklet for children, so he told the story of Rudolph the Red-Nosed Reindeer. That same year, Gene Autrey recorded the song we know and love today, and Santa's nine reindeer have been pulling his sleigh on Christmas Eve ever since.

Coca-Cola Santa

Although the story of Santa Claus, Saint Nick or Father Christmas had been told for centuries around the world, it was only in 1931 that the jolly and jovial picture of Santa Claus came to be. That year, Coca-Cola was looking for a star character to lead the company's Christmas ad campaign. They enlisted the help of Haddon Sundblom, a talented illustrator of the 1930s. Sundblom found illustrations of St. Nicholas and stumbled upon Clement C. Moore's poem "The Night Before Christmas." Drawing inspiration from this gift-giving character, Sundblom began to develop his idea. Up until that point, images of Santa depicted a tall, gaunt man or a small elvish character, always dressed in a variety of cloth-

> *He imparted a sense of warmth with a frostbitten pink nose and rosy cheeks.*

ing. Sundblom decided on a color palette of red and white — Coca-Cola's colors — and used his friend Lou Prentice as a model. He dressed Santa in a warm fur-lined coat to protect him against snowy nights and imparted realism and a sense of warmth with a frostbitten pink nose and rosy cheeks, twinkling eyes, a broad smile and a round belly. Coca-Cola armed jolly St. Nick with a refreshing Coke in hand. The company then began a broad and successful advertising campaign for the new and improved Santa. The appeal and popularity of this cheerful Santa sky-rocketed throughout America. Proving to be a popular image, Sundblom's drawings changed the way Santa has been depicted forever, leaving a legacy for years to come.

Legends

Just as personal stories bring beloved family heirlooms to life, rich legends and folklore enhance the magic of classic holiday tales.

The Cardinal

Few Christmastime visuals are as striking as the vibrant red feathers of a cardinal contrasting with a dusting of white snow. Because of their spectacular scarlet color, cardinals have become a symbol of the beauty and warmth of the holiday season. It is said that they represent loved ones who have passed and are coming to visit. Decorating with cardinal figurines can keep the spirit of loved ones close during the holiday season.

Cardinals are known to appear when you need to feel close to the person you miss. Sometimes they fly near in times of celebration, reminding us that our loved ones are always with us in spirit. It is said that if you look for a cardinal, one will appear right when you need it, as though it was sent from the heavens.

Symbolizing a visit from a loved
one, a flock of red clip-on
cardinal ornaments stands out
against a festive preserved
boxwood wreath.

The Poinsettia

The poinsettia's association with Christmas began one cold Christmas Eve long ago. A poor young child was walking down the street to Church, weeping in sadness because they could not afford a gift to offer to baby Jesus. As the child wept, an angel appeared from the heavens. The angel instructed the child to pick a nearby weed and carry it to the Church as an offering instead of a gift, telling the child, "It's not what you give, but what you give of your heart." Having faith in the angel, the child took the unassuming weed and stepped into the church. Upon walking in the door, the ugly weed suddenly bloomed into a gorgeous red poinsettia, becoming a worthy gift for baby Jesus.

Beyond their rich history, poinsettias have symbolic significance, too. The star shape of their signature flower represents the star of Bethlehem, their red color represents the blood of Christ, and white flowers represent his purity. Symbolizing warmth and love, poinsettias brighten holiday decor with their vibrant red flowers, and they are a great way to warm your interior environment.

Upon walking in the door, the ugly weed suddenly bloomed into a gorgeous red poinsettia, becoming a worthy gift for baby Jesus.

Icicles

Icicles are more than just majestic wintertime phenomena. As the story goes, on a bitter cold winter night, a snowstorm raged through a forest. A stranded child wandered through the wilderness seeking shelter from the blizzard. He came upon the sturdy, bowing branches of a fir tree and crept beneath the thick boughs, hoping they would shield him from the elements. The fir faced the winds with all its strength, vowing to protect the boy no matter how long the storm ensued. The next morning when the clouds parted and the sun shone again, the boy emerged and thanked the fir for protecting him. It was then that the fir learned the boy was the Christ child, and the tree wept tears of joy for the honor of protecting him. As tears dripped down the boughs, they froze upon the branches as icicles, glistening like diamonds in the winter sun. Every Christmas, the firs weep again, creating icicles in memory of this holy time. Around the home, glass icicle ornaments of different sizes, shapes and patterns create a diverse homage to the fir tree's holy sacrifice.

The Pickle

Many Christmas traditions were created with children in mind, and the Christmas Pickle is one of them. The custom began as a German tradition and has been passed down for many years. On Christmas Eve as children are fast asleep, parents hide a small glass pickle ornament deep within the tree. In the morning, as the family gathers to open gifts, the children search high and low for the pickle. The child who finds the ornament gets a special gift that Santa leaves the night before, and the recipient has good fortune in the coming year. The tradition lives on as a way for families to have a little fun on Christmas morning.

Tinsel and the Christmas Tree

Eastern European tradition is to thank for the shimmering strands of tinsel adorning our Christmas trees today. As the story goes, a woman cleaned and decorated her whole house for Christmas. The spiders of the house wanted a closer look at the beautiful tree with its colorful decorations, so they gathered together to inspect it. They were so overjoyed when they saw the tree up close that they danced across its branches in celebration, spinning gossamer webs as they went. That night, Father Christmas climbed down the chimney and discovered the shining webs covering the tree. Enchanted by their beauty and knowing the woman had spent a long time cleaning, he turned the webs into beautiful strands of silver and gold tinsel. To this day, beautifully decorated trees worldwide are celebrated with shimmering strands of tinsel draped across their branches.

The Robin

While many of our native birds fly south for the winter, robins from Scandinavia, Russia and Europe flock to the United States where food is more abundant in the winter. These red-breasted birds have naturally become symbols of winter, but they have a rich religious symbolism as well. At the first Christmas, the fire keeping Mary warm as she gave birth began to dim. Shivering and cold, Mary called out to a nearby robin for help. Recognizing the importance of this moment, the robin gathered sticks and twigs to add to the fire, and he gallantly flew close to the flames, using its tiny wings to fan the embers. As the fire grew, the heat of the embers burned the robin's breast, turning it as red as the flames themselves. The robin built the fire up until it was warm enough to heat the cold stable and keep Mary and the baby Jesus warm. Mary declared that the robin's breast would always remain red as a reminder of his brave deed, and the robin's descendants wear the red breast proudly as a symbol of their compassion and kindness.

Over the years, robins have also come to represent postal carriers. Artists illustrated robins delivering Christmas cards to snow-covered mailboxes, and you might see them adorning mailboxes and postcards around the Christmas season as a nod to the tradition.

Birds Nest

According to German legend, if you find a bird's nest in the Christmas tree you harvest, you will have good luck and prosperity all year long. Nests represent the love, commitment and effort that it takes to build a sturdy and happy home. Birds' nest ornaments are a lasting reminder of warmth and devotion around the holidays, and they can be symbols of good luck when nestled among your tree's branches.

If you find a bird's nest in the Christmas tree you harvest, you will have good luck all year long.

Traditions

Colorful customs and Christmas traditions enrich holiday celebrations and add an extra-special touch to the season.

Flaked coconut makes a soft white bed of snow for festive Santa sugar cookies.

Cookies for Santa

The tradition of leaving cookies for Santa wasn't always a sweet intention. Beginning sometime in the 1930s, naughty children would leave cookies out as an attempt to appeal to Santa on Christmas Eve. They feared waking up to an empty tree the next morning and began leaving treats as a bribe. Eventually, well behaved children also started using cookies, but they left sweets as a way to thank Santa for all of his hard work. To this day children leave treats for Santa and his reindeer before they go to bed in hopes of waking up to an empty cookie plate and a stocking full of gifts.

Caroling

A joyous crowd of Christmas carolers is a universal sign of holiday cheer. However, the custom didn't begin with Christmas in mind. In 19th century London, a young girl named Carol Poles went missing during the holiday season. A large group of townspeople mobilized to find Carol, and they began going door to door to look for her. To declare their good intentions,

To declare their good intentions, the search party began to sing.

the search parties began to sing songs as they walked so as not to frighten people when the crowd approached their homes. In honor of Carol's memory, the tradition carried on and came to be called caroling. Over the years it has taken on a happier note, with carolers spreading Christmas joy door to door with their holiday tunes.

Gingerbread

There are few scents that instantly transport you to the warm feelings of Christmas like gingerbread does. The tradition started in Germany, where gingersnap cookies have long been associated with the holiday season. It wasn't until the early 1800s that bakers began to use holiday gingerbread to build extravagant fairytale houses. The confections had a variety of artistic depictions, gilded details and German architectural features. The practice of making gingerbread houses spread through America with the arrival of German immigrants, and soon after, the tradition took off worldwide and has since become synonymous with the Christmas season.

Gingersnap Cookies

Preparation Time: 25 minutes
Yields: 7 dozen
Ingredients:

2 cups all-purpose flour

¼ teaspoon salt

2 teaspoons baking soda

1 teaspoon cinnamon

1 teaspoon ground ginger

1 teaspoon ground cloves

¾ cup vegetable shortening

1½ cups sugar, divided

1 egg

¼ cup light or dark molasses

Directions:

Preheat the oven to 350°F. Sift flour, salt, baking soda and spices together in a bowl. Set aside. In a separate bowl, cream shortening and one cup sugar until light and fluffy. Add egg and molasses, mixing until combined. Gradually blend in sifted ingredients. Dough will be very sticky. Roll into walnut-sized balls. Dip in ½ cup sugar and place on cookie sheets, allowing room to spread. Bake for 8 to 10 minutes. Finger should leave a slight indentation in the cookie when it's done. Avoid overbaking.

Oranges

Oranges have always been a special Christmastime treat. Before produce was as widely available as it is today, oranges were costly and scarce in the wintertime in many regions. They developed a reputation as a winter delicacy in some cultures. Santa would often leave one of these fresh, juicy fruits in the toes of stockings to reward good behavior. Oranges were such a widely regarded winter delicacy that they were some of the first glass ornaments ever made, enhancing and adorning the earliest Christmas trees. This seasonal delicacy has worked its way into holiday decor, providing a vibrant pop of color to wintertime arrangements.

Fresh oranges and glass ornaments bring unexpected flair to non-traditional colors and striking combinations of textures.

Debbie's Orange Balls

Preparation Time: 30 minutes

Yields: 4 dozen

Ingredients:

1 11-ounce box vanilla wafers, crushed

3½ cups confectioners' sugar, plus more for rolling

1 6-ounce can frozen orange juice concentrate, thawed

¼ cup melted butter

1 cup chopped pecans

Directions:

Combine all ingredients in a bowl, mixing them well. Form into small balls and roll in additional confectioners' sugar to coat. Store in an airtight covered container or freeze until ready to serve.

A limited edition Chalkware Santa designed by Vaillancourt Folk Art Co. for The Thicket stands beside oak tree imagery to symbolize strength and good luck.

Acorns

As the saying goes, "From a tiny acorn sprang the mighty oak." The mighty oak tree is cherished as a symbol of strength. Its acorns are considered good luck charms because they bear within them the beginnings of tall, towering trees. The oak is so prized, it is America's national tree, and in German custom, oaks are considered sacred. Oak leaves and acorns have become strong symbols in these cultures. Early German Christmas trees were covered in acorns to commemorate the gift of life and to bring about luck. Around the world, acorns can still be found as ornaments and decorations, representing strength and luck.

Walnuts

At Christmastime, bowls of walnuts and nutcrackers adorn holiday tables around the world, but the nuts aren't just for snacking. These holiday symbols have a history dating back to early Christmas celebrations. St. Nick traditionally left walnuts in stockings as treats for children. During the Victorian era, walnuts were used to decorate the Christmas tree. They adorned branches along with raisins, fruits and popcorn. However, these were no ordinary nuts. The shells were often gilded with gold leaf and hung on the tree with a red bow, and many times people would hide trinkets inside the shells. Walnuts were also some of the first objects to be reproduced as glass ornaments

A plentiful walnut harvest was frequently associated with the birth of more children the following year, so walnuts became a good luck charm and were scattered on the ground at weddings and winter holiday celebrations to bring about good fortune. Today, the long history of the walnut continues. Walnuts appear in baked goods, alongside nutcrackers and in edible displays as timeless symbols of the season.

Pinecones

Just as evergreens are stunning natural icons of the holiday season, pinecones are also notable natural Christmas decorations. These seed-bearing cones are symbols of motherhood and new life. Many times, brides were given pinecones on their wedding day to hang on their trees. Not only do pinecones represent new life, the seeds within them also provide food for birds and animals throughout the winter months. Because of their integral role in the life cycle of the forest, pinecones were some of earliest objects made into glass ornaments. Whether used in their natural form or as ornaments, pinecones are always a timeless favorite during the holiday season.

Mixed textures like moss, a wire nest and glass come together to tell a colorful and bright story of birds nesting in the forest.

Birds

One cannot think of the splendor of Christmas trees without thinking of the vibrant birds that perch upon them. Birds are a universal symbol of joy and happiness, and many believe that every tree must have a bird ornament on it. Glassblowers who made early ornaments often collected live birds so they could more accurately replicate their plumage. The artists kept the birds not only for inspiration, but also for the joyous tunes they would sing in response to the sound of the Bunsen burners' gas flames.

Because the process of creating glass ornaments was painstaking and difficult, very few glassblowers mastered the craft, and original bird ornaments were quite rare. Today, many collectors have memories of these birds hanging on their grandmothers' trees, which has driven demand for these rare collectors items to this day. Birds, whether caged in a whimsical arrangement or freely perched among ornaments on the tree, continue to be popular for the messages of love and good fortune that they represent.

A natural tree branch
extending from the
Christmas tree provides
a perfect perch for a
collection of clip-on
bird ornaments.

Pear Tree

The partridge in a pear tree is the culmination of the "12 Days of Christmas" and has commonly come to be associated with Christmas day. According to the song, the season actually starts on Christmas day and extends to the 11 days following the 25th. The song is believed to be a memory game song and originated in France around 1780. It first appeared in a children's book called *Mirth With-out Mischief*. Each day is a metaphor for a Bible story about God's love, and the partridge represents Jesus because, like Christ, it will sacrifice its life to save its children. In *The Odyssey,* the Greek poet Homer acclaims pears as a "gift of the gods." This might be why the song describes the partridge in a pear tree, but no one knows for sure. Its origin aside, the "12 Days of Christmas" immortalized pears in popular culture, solidifying their role as a representation of the Christmas season.

Elements like fresh and ornamental pears along with a nesting partridge pay homage to the "12 Days of Christmas" in a dessert buffet.

A small partridge nestled in
a pear tree is accompanied
by two larger partridge
figurines on the buffet and
pears tucked into the table
centerpiece.

Pear Honey

Ingredients:
4 cups pears, peeled and ground
4 cups sugar
1 cup crushed pineapple

Directions:
In a saucepan over medium heat, cook all ingredients until mixture is clear and thick.

Mushrooms

Mushrooms have long been a symbol of good luck in German culture. They can be found sprouting up from lush, green European forests, and they're often associated with the nature, beauty and mystery of the forest. To find a mushroom in the forest is considered good fortune, much like finding a lucky penny or a four-leaf clover. Because of this, children often scour the woods in hopes of discovering a double mushroom — two mushroom tops growing from the same stem — for even more luck. As decorations and ornaments, mushrooms bring good fortune into the home and represent hopes of prosperity for the coming year, which is why to this day, mushrooms are still found on nearly every Christmas tree in Germany.

Paperwhite Narcissus

Paperwhite narcissus, most commonly referred to as paperwhites, are December's birth flower. It's a fitting choice, as the bright white flower is one of the few narcissus varieties to bloom in the winter. It's the perfect flower to represent the Christmas season, as it's also easy to grow indoors. Many families traditionally grow paperwhites during the holidays because it is said that watching new life grow through the winter brings hope for the coming spring. Seeing the blooms gradually emerge is also a reminder to slow down during the hectic holiday season. Once bloomed, paperwhites have long, skinny stems and clusters of tiny white blossoms. These fresh white blossoms with their concentrated musky scent can bring bright life to any room during the drab winter months.

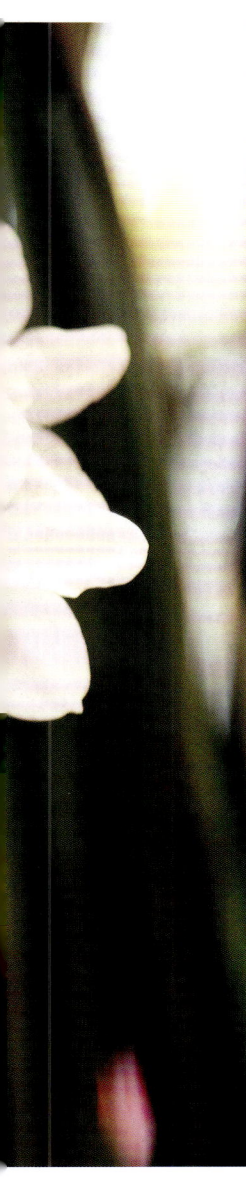

The paperwhite's long, reedy stems of white blossoms can be held upright by tall glass vases.

How To Force
Paperwhites

1 Approximately three weeks before you want them to bloom, place the bulbs right-side up among pebbles in a glass vase. The roots will be the only element of the bulb below the surface of the water.

2 Water so that only the roots and underside of the bulb get wet. Keep the water level consistent and do not submerge the bulb more than halfway.

3 Place your paperwhites in a cool room with strong indirect sunlight

4 Clusters of fragrant white blossoms will appear in about three weeks.

*Place your paperwhites
in a cool room with
strong indirect sunlight*

Fresh white rose petals create a soft bed of snow beneath Santa as he emerges from the forest in this cookie buffet accented with glass trees, red fruit ornaments and cake stands.

Cookie Buffets

Although it may seem like a modern way to spread holiday cheer, sharing Christmas cookies is an age-old tradition with European roots. As people migrated around the world, so did their cookie-baking customs. Some of the earliest cookies in America date back to Dutch immigrants from the 1600s. The cookie buffet embodies the youthful spirit of the holidays. Piles of sweet treats along with plates of confections are a great way to share cherished family recipes and decadent desserts we look forward to all season. Cake stands stacked high with mountains of Christmas cookies create what feels like a holiday smorgasbord that can instantly draw guests in.

Arranging the delicacies on trays and dessert stands in a variety of heights makes your tablescape more visually interesting. Combining elements like trees, ornaments and Santas adds interest and a sense of magic to the decadent spread.

Glittery red strawberry ornaments and snow-like white rose petals draw attention to jam-filled thumbprints and frosted snowflake cookies.

Candy Strawberries

Ingredients:
1 6-ounce box strawberry Jell-O
¾ cup sweetened condensed milk
Dash of salt
1 cup finely chopped pecans
½ teaspoon vanilla extract
1 cup shredded sweetened coconut
Red and green colored sugar

Directions:
In a bowl, mix all ingredients except colored sugar and chill. Form into strawberry shaped balls. Place red and green sugar in separate bowls. Roll candies in red sugar and top with green sugar. Chill until serving time.

Marshmallow Deer

During the Christmas season, it isn't as much about the decorations themselves as it is about the love that goes into them. That's why you'll find handmade Popsicle stick ornaments adorning parents' Christmas trees, or grandma's chipped holiday plates on the buffets of her grandchildren's homes. Adding handmade elements to decor conveys a unique personal touch. For example, this candy deer makes a show-stopping appearance on a cookie buffet, but the attention to detail that went into making it serves as the true wow-factor. Made by painstakingly gluing mini marshmallows to a deer form, Rudolph stands proudly among other treats knowing he is the finest of them all.

Rudolph's striking antlers were made by wiring red Twizzlers to the deer form, and his holly wreath adornments are spearmint gumdrops and red candies.

Scattered mini marshmallows represent a bed of soft snow beneath Santa cookies and a flower-filled glass boot.

Candy Dishes

Beyond holding sweet treats, candy dishes can be a great opportunity to turn an otherwise generic dish into an eye-catching composition. Simple, unexpected touches and whimsical details can turn ordinary into extraordinary. A pair of ruby red cardinals peering into a green leaf-shaped dish give the impression of a treasure trove found in the woods. This is also a great place to showcase cherished ornaments that would otherwise get lost hanging on a tree. A candy dish can be anchored with an intricate figurine placed proudly among metallic-wrapped candies. Glass ornaments with the caps gently removed can be repurposed as playful bud vases, which bring a fresh floral element to an otherwise ordinary dish. Thoughtfully adding ornaments and figurines to candy dishes is an easy way to breathe the Christmas spirit into your home while giving the eye something sweet to take in, too.

By gently removing the caps from ornaments, they can be used as bud vases or set among festive candies. This draws attention to your favorite ornaments that might get lost buried deep within the tree.

A metallic-themed candy dish recreates the shimmering magic of a shining star with elements like mercury glass dishes, metallic garland and reflective stars in the shape of the star of Bethlehem.

Fireplace Mantels

In any room, the fireplace is a natural focal point, and it serves as a warm and welcoming gathering space in the cold winter months. Therefore, the fireplace mantel is a perfect place to create a magical Christmas story. Not only does this draw the eye to your room's best feature, but it also sets the tone for the room's holiday decor. Using elements of different shapes and sizes to create visual interest helps makes the most of the space, starting with taller items in the back and smaller items in the front to give your arrangement beautiful dimension. Elements that complement each other in style, color or theme create a cohesive mantelscape. Pay careful attention to proportions — balance doesn't mean that all pieces have to match. You can have several small, thin, or light items on one side balanced with one visually heavy item on the other side. Keeping in mind the story you're trying to tell with your arrangement allows you to have fun trying out different layouts until you create something you really love.

A red and green color scheme is elevated with rustic evergreen elements, antique trophies and an explosion of bright red tulips.

A cheeky nod to its history, an antique Rose Bowl Trophy from
a European Rose Society is filled with fresh red roses.

Rustic bark candles nestled in moss add glow to this grouping of evergreens.

Game trophies, boxwood topiaries along with fresh
woodland greenery and an antique deer watch holder
create a warm lodge feeling.

Remember that nothing is permanent. You can always move things around and play with the setup.

Natural pine cone elements along with antler and mercury glass candle holders bring rustic elegance to this grouping framing a watercolor elk painting.

Outdoor elements like a concrete statue, boxwoods and fresh white roses create the sense of walking through a winter garden.

A playful arrangement of glass finials create the impression of church steeples peering over the horizon of a snow covered hill.

Ventorati Potivs
ONOCLEA SENSIBILIS

ONOCLEA

Simple wooden rods stuck in floral foam help to keep finials standing upright.

A pair of antique Staffordshire dog figurines always looks classic and polished.

An antique oak leaf and acorn majolica dish creates a focal point in this mantelscape. An antique water filter exploding with lush winter berries and fragrant evergreens anchors the composition, and glass ornaments add a bit of sparkle.

Mossy branches gathered from a walk in the woods create the perfect thicket for a collection of colorful clip-on bird ornaments.

A spruce bough dripping with icicles creates a canopy over a vibrant village alive with color. Layering icicles in front of the mirror doubles the dramatic effect of the sparkling glass.

*Depth is created
by layering
items in front of
each other.*

A swagging spruce bough provides shelter for the vibrant village below. Glistening icicles draw attention to the glittery dusting of snow on the trees and buildings.

Contrasting textures like natural moss and smooth, clear glass create a magical mantelscape, and the candlelight adds elegance with a soft glow.

Vaillancourt 12 Days
of Christmas Santa
ornaments become a
showcase when layered
atop deep green plates.

The Details

When it comes to decorating for Christmas, it really is all about those tiny elements that make your decorations sing. We hear it all the time, "the design is in the details," and adding lush layers to a collection of majolica plates can draw the eye right where you want it to go. Vaillancourt Santa ornaments in a 12 Days of Christmas theme become much more noticeable when layered on top of deep green plates, and a small sprig of greenery tied with a bright ribbon adds another layer of detail to discover. Layering elements, varying textures and considering every detail creates a dynamic composition for highlighting your favorite ornaments.

Vaillancourt chalkware Santas and antique deer are encapsulated beneath snow globe–like glass cloches, which lend a sense of importance to themed groupings.

Ordinary table salt makes great snow. It's easy to source, and it serves as a shimmery and firm base for composing wintry snow-dusted scenes.

Vintage Christmas characters are nestled in a wintry white bed of table salt to create a snowy scene atop decorative cake stands.

Pinecone branches support the heavy blooms of the amaryllis. Woodland-inspired greenery in the deer cigar holder ties the forest grouping together.

A wood tray anchors this collection of wildlife-inspired antiques, and fresh tulips elevate the mood and inject life and fresh energy into winter decor.

The mixture of textures of glass, ornaments and flowers make a dynamic arrangement accented by the subtle glow of lit candles. An added base of moss holds ornaments and candles in place.

The combination of fresh flowers and greenery with fruit-inspired ornaments evokes the sense (and smell!) of walking through a winter garden, creating a unique sensory experience.

Reflective glass ornaments in zesty green create a contrast of textures when paired with a combination of green cymbidium orchids, hydrangea and fragrant evergreens.

ATHYRIUM FILIX

Combining textures of various types of trees, whether bottle brush, glass or molded, creates a richness in tabletop groupings.

An antique peppermint jar serves as the perfect vessel for a combination of red winter berries, star of Bethlehem, and mini peppermint carnations.

When considering the details, make sure all cherished family members are included. Oaks the mini goldendoodle has his own Christmas tree, decorated with a limited edition paw print ornament he made himself and his own collection of ornaments.

Happy Holidays

The Johnsons
Ron, Debbie and Oaks

happy holidays

Ron, Debbie and Oaks

merry
THE JOHNSONS
Ron, Debbie and Oaks

About the Author

Ron Johnson is a self-taught floral designer and Christmas enthusiast who draws inspiration from nature. He has been in the floral and home decor industry since he was 16 years old and has turned his eye for detail and his passion for design into a career. Ron lives in Springfield, Missouri, with his wife, Debbie, and his best friend and four-legged companion Oaks. Ron and Debbie are the owners of three specialty shops. Their stores The Thicket and Branches both specialize in home decor and seasonal accents, and The Nest is a floral shop that carries fresh flowers and garden decor.

surfa
into a
side, cut
center.

on the
day of
RISTMAS

PEPP